My Pet is Sick- I have to say goodbye

Jill A. Johnson-Young, LCSW

ISBN-13: 978-0-9997886-3-9

LIBRARY OF CONGRESS CONTROL NUMBER:2019914963

DEDICATION

This book is dedicated to the memory of the furpersons who spent their lifetimes with me, whose warm noses and loving eyes provided a safe place to share secrets and thoughts, to share happiness and victories, and offered a warm and loving place to grieve. I want to especially remember my childhood companion, Piggy, referred to by my dad as "the best gentleman cat who ever lived;" my college and grad school purrperson, Truffles, who made the long days and nights better. I apologize Truff, for having to use catnip to finish my MSW; The most amazing rescue Akita ever, Maggie, who gently and playfully caught my heart when I lost my Sandy dog; Princess, the puppy of my children's childhood; Fuzzy, the Oodle who stole hearts wherever she went, despite cataracts that eventually stole her sight, and spent her days caring for grieving clients and family members as they faced the end of their lives. Finally, a special note for Lexie, the blind and deaf rescue Oodle, who came home to us for the last six months of her life. She somehow trusted us to keep her safe and to provide the snuggles she deserved, and in doing so found a place in my heart forever.

I want to thank Hannah Stacie Reedy, for being my partner in Oodle rescuing, and for helping in so many ways with every book- without the thanks she so deserves.

I would like to thank the staff at Valley Animal Hospital who provide loving care for our Oodles, send us home with new rescues, who help our oldest pets leave this world in loving arms with gentle voices, and even a few tears – and not just mine.

Finally, this book is dedicated to the veterinarians who make this world a better place. You take care of all the creatures great and small. You work long hours and are far less appreciated than you deserve. You are frequently left alone to hold furry family members as they draw their last breaths when the family does not want to be present, which makes for so many emotionally draining moments that none of us are ever aware of when we walk through your doors and you greet our pets with a smile and reassurance. Thank you from all of us who count on you. I hope this book will help your families see that side of your work, and to prepare better for those moments so they will stay present when the end of life comes for their furry family members.

My Pet Is Sick- I Have to Say Goodbye

ACKNOWLEDGMENTS

Grief and loss are part of life for all of us. Normalizing talking with our children about losing a loved one or a beloved pet when they die rather than shielding kiddos from the reality of death prepares them for coping with loss as adults. I receive calls at my office asking if parents should simply tell a child that their dog or cat (or lizard, snake, hamster, Guinea pig, turtle, even goldfish) ran away or found a new family rather than allowing them to grieve a pet who died. Sometimes they want to know if they should tell a child that Grandma died. What is the child supposed to think? Everyone they ever loved, including grandma, wanted to run away from them? Loss hurts- but we can teach kiddos to cope. That is a skill all of us need in this life.

I was fortunate to grow up in a home where we attended funerals as small children, celebrated cat birthdays with tuna fish cakes, and buried our pets in the backyard with services we were encouraged to create ourselves. I can still remember my dad's "funeral suit" and the feeling of its soft material when I leaned against him at cemeteries. My kids, and now my grandkids, have had the same experiences. When we make death a part of life and teach them to remember those who died and to talk about them to keep them with us in our hearts, loss is not so sad or scary. They learn that death does not mean someone they loved will disappear, and that it is okay to make them a part of the rest of their lives.

I hope this book will help the Big People reading it to their Little People normalize the loss of a pet. That it will create a dialogue about death and life in your family that they will carry into adulthood. I want it to help you welcome home a new rescue after you have grieved, one who needs your love as much as the one you lost. Our pets spend their whole lifetime with us. We have room in our lifetimes to share that love again after we have said goodbye, while never forgetting those who are forever in our hearts.

MY PET IS SICK.

I am worried.

We have always been together.

I can't remember a time when my pet was not waiting at home for me to get home.

When I have a bad day, I can tell him about it.

When I have an argument with my friends my pet makes the day better.

On good days we celebrate together.

But today when I got home from school, my pet did not meet me.

I had to go find him.

He didn't wag his tail for me.

He didn't want to lick my face.

I laid down next to him.

I tried to make him snuggle. He didn't
seem to want to.

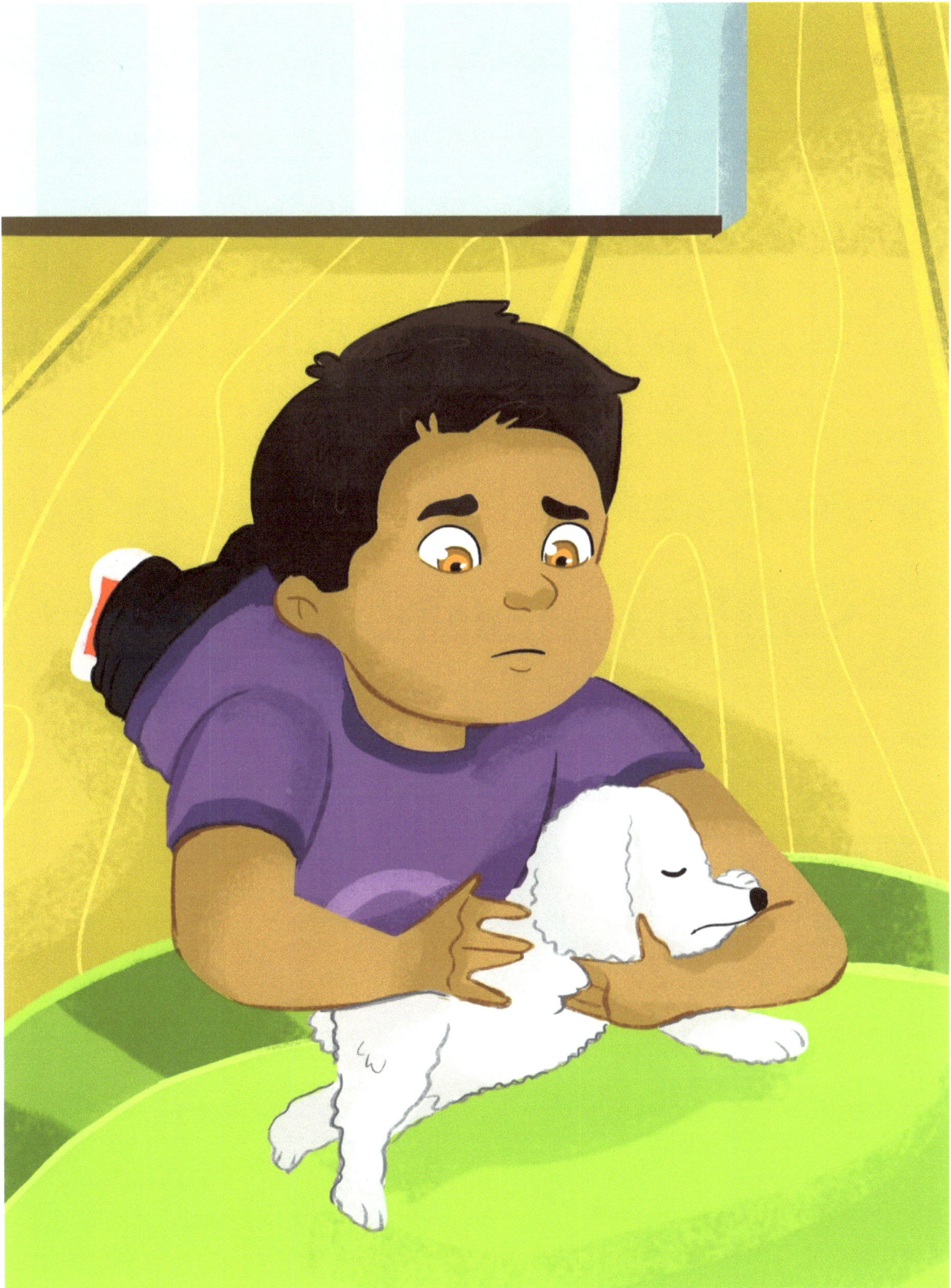

I told my parents, and they called our veterinarian.

She said to come in right away.

We bundled him up in a soft blanket, and he sat next to me in the car.

He laid his head in my hand.

When we got to the veterinarian, her helper met us and took us into a room to see the doctor.

Even in her purple hair she looked worried.

Usually she smiles and ruffles my pet's fur. Today she looked sad and stroked him instead.

They took blood samples, and his temperature, and examined him. He didn't even argue about the needle.

I saw my mom step out of the room with the doctor.

Her helper stayed with me and we petted and stroked him, and she told him he was a good boy, and how much she had always liked him.

When they came back, they both had tears in their eyes.

The doctor bent over a little to look at me and said that sometimes she can't fix what's wrong.

She said that she could not make him get well.

There was no medicine that would help.

We stood there for a bit, and then mom said we could take him home and let him die there, but the doctor told her that it would not feel good to him.

She talked about the Rainbow Bridge, and my pet being able to run over it soon and feel well and happy again.

She said he would always know how much I loved him.

I asked what would happen. The doctor explained that we were going to put him to sleep. She would give him a medicine to make him relax, and then sleep, and then another medicine that would let him die gently and safely with me holding him. She promised it would not hurt him.

She asked if I was okay with that, or if I needed time to get ready, and come back tomorrow.

She said he would not feel good tonight if we did that, but she would understand.

Mom and I hugged him and petted him, and we said it was okay.

They lit a special candle in the front of the office, to tell other people that this was happening.

The helper brought in a big furry blanket, and we put him on it, while mom and I held him.

In a minute he was relaxing, then sleeping. Then he was so relaxed I could feel him relaxing into my arms.

A few minutes later he stopped breathing.

The doctor checked him carefully. She petted him. She still looked so sad- and we were all crying.

She said he was gone- he was on the Rainbow Bridge.

Mom and I took his collar and kissed him goodbye.

They said they would cremate him and we could come get him in a week to take home.

It was so quiet in the car.

Mom asked me what my favorite memories were of him. We talked about chasing balls, about him stealing food from my plate, about sleeping next to each other, and him unwrapping presents on holidays when he found them on the floor.

Mom told me we were really lucky to find someone who we could love so much, and who loved us right back. She said someday we would find someone else and share the love he gave us. Right now, we needed to have time to say goodbye, because he was irreplaceable.

I had a big hole in my heart when we walked in the door and he wasn't there.

Bedtime was hard because he was not on my bed. Waking up I had to remember he died.

We talked about him a lot, and that helped.

I told my friends, and they talked about their pets who died too.

My grandma sent a card to tell me how much she knew I loved him, and how sad she was that he died.

And then a wooden box came with his ashes in it, and a footprint on clay, and a little of his fur. My mom put it on the fireplace mantle. I put the footprint next to my bed.

Now before bed I can hold it and remember him, and how much I will always love him.

And I think about him running, and playing, and feeling good, and wagging his tail.

I am glad he was mine, and always will be part of me.

<u>Helps for the Big People</u>

I wrote this book at the request of parents and our own veterinarian.

When we have pets in our families it is inevitable that they will eventually die. If we talk our children through that, and give them the chance to understand it, we teach them how to manage grief. They will learn that death is a part of life, and that they can love someone, lose them, and keep them with them for the rest of their lives. We can teach them to talk about who they miss, and what they meant to them. Pets are a big part of family life for many of us, and their deaths should be honored and their memories shared.

If you have a sick pet:

- **Let your children go with you to the vet. They will see you are trying to help them.**
- **Let them hear what the doctor is saying, on their developmental level.**
- **If it is simply an illness, let them experience a vet helping their pet get well again.**
- **If it is time to put a pet to sleep, then let them be part of that, too.**
- **I realize many adults feel that they cannot be present when a pet is being put to sleep, but if your kids are with you, it is time to make yourself plant your feet firmly on the ground and stay present.**
- **You can, and should, cry. Model that for your child.**
- **Let them pet, and stroke, and cry.**

- Do not rush them out afterward. Let them take time to say goodbye, and to collect themselves.

- Have the cremated remains returned, so you can have some sort of ceremony.

- Allow them to speak, just as you would at a funeral. Your pet has died- this is a funeral.

- Say your pet's name often, and out loud. It gives your children the permission they need to talk, even if it makes you sad.

- Do not run out and get a new pet right away. We do not want to teach kids that anyone is replaceable, and that replacing fixes loss. It doesn't- it masks it.

- When it is time to find a new pet, do not look for a twin. New people come into our lives when others die, and the same goes for pets. They do not look alike. They do not share a name.

- Consider an ornament for the holidays or a special picture on the wall to hold a special place for your furry family member's place in your lives.

ABOUT THE AUTHOR

Jill Johnson-Young, LCSW is the CEO of Central Counseling Services in Riverside and Murrieta, California. She's a certified Grief Recovery Facilitator and specializes in grief and loss, dementia, trauma, and adoption issues. She spent more than a decade with hospice, including pediatric hospice and children's grief programming. Jill is a nationally known speaker on death and dying, dementia, and grief and loss, engaging her audience with humor and a message that grief does not have to last forever.

Jill holds a BA from the University of California, Riverside and her MSW from the University of South Florida. She has authored two other books about grief for children, "Someone is sick- how do I say goodbye?" and "Someone I love just died- what happens now?" She has also authored a workbook for grief for adults, "Your Own Path Through Grief," and has several more books coming. Jill created Your Path Through Grief, a year-long, comprehensive grief support program for those who are not likely to attend a grief support group, which includes pages for therapists and resources for anyone who might need them. Jill's goal is to get us all talking about death as a part of life, grief as a normal experience, and to make those subjects accessible for all ages. The Oodles would like to add that if her work convinces a few people to rescue a midlife, senior, or special needs pet along the way it will make everything worthwhile.

www.ingramcontent.com/pod-product-compliance
Lightning Source LLC
Chambersburg PA
CBHW061056090426
42742CB00002B/62